Catherine Bisset

Placeholder

Salamander Street

PLAYS

Placeholder was performed as a solo show and takes as its starting point the idea that the gaps in the archives, and absence of enslaved voices in the texts, are themselves acts of suppression.

Placeholder had its premiere at the Scottish Storytelling Centre in Edinburgh in November 2021, as part of the Being Human Festival programme and a second performance at the Byre Theatre in St Andrews in February 2022. Running at approximately 60 minutes, both performances were livestreamed and included a Q&A with the creative team and Julia Prest, Professor of French and Caribbean Studies at the University of St Andrews.

Placeholder was written and performed by Catherine Bisset, with dramaturgy by Jaïrus Obayomi and directed by Flavia D'Avila under the banner of her Edinburgh-based production company, Fronteiras Theatre Lab. This project was inspired by research conduted by Professor Julia Prest and The Colonial-Era Caribbean Theatre and Opera Network (CECTON) network and kindly supported by a Research Network Grant from the Royal Society of Edinburgh and the Collaboration, Research and Development Fund of the City of Edinburgh Council.

For mum and dad.

With special thanks to

Donald, Daniel and Amy for their love and patience. Flavia and Jaïrus for their creative brilliance in bringing my words to life. Professor Julia Prest and the CECTON network whose important research informed and inspired me. Jen McGregor for her kind and invaluable advice and Mark Bolsover for his expert proof-reading. Rebecca Fairnie and Angela Milton for their insightful feedback on the early draft and support exactly when I needed it, Edinburgh Acting School (EAS) for starting me on this journey and for their unwavering encouragement and Lucy and everyone at Salamander Street for their belief in the play.

ABOUT CATHERINE BISSET

Catherine Bisset is an Edinburgh-based actor and playwright, whose Jamaican-Scottish ancestry is reflected in her love of telling and writing stories that reach across cultures and histories.

After 20 years working as a justice analyst for the Scottish Government she stumbled into the world of theatre after taking up acting as a weekly hobby, and has never left, being lucky enough to perform in a number of plays thanks to the expert training and encouragement she received at Edinburgh Acting School. Through acting, Catherine developed a passion for Knowledge-Exchange theatre, in particular how playwrights can give voices to those who are absent from the history books and official texts.

Placeholder, Catherine's first play, was long-listed for an Alfred Fagon Award in 2022 and came runner up in the 'Production of the Year' category in the Framework Theatre Awards for emerging writers in 2021.

When Catherine isn't acting, writing or researching, she can be found sipping wine in her wee cottage on the beautiful Isle of Skye.

Q&A WITH DIRECTOR FLAVIA D'AVILA
AND PLAYWRIGHT CATHERINE BISSET

Flavia: This wasn't the first time we've worked together. I'd directed you in the Edinburgh Acting School (EAS) production of *Lysistrata*, but how was this experience different for you?

Catherine: It was pretty different especially as *Placeholder* was such an intense and involved project, but both were fantastically creative experiences. *Lysistrata* was a straight acting role, but I got to know your collaborative directing style and observed how well you worked with actors. You yanked me out of my comfort zone with *Placeholder*, though. The first conversation we had was over Zoom and I remember you said something like, 'You fancy writing a play?' and I responded, 'Er, well, I've never written anything longer than a work email but I'll give it a go.' I tried to play it super-cool but inside I was absolutely petrified and had no idea why you asked me to do it!

It was only later that I discovered that Jen McGregor (writer, director and EAS tutor) had suggested that I might be up for it based on a short piece of writing I'd done for her writing course. In addition, it transpired my Jamaican heritage was relevant to the brief and I already knew quite a bit about slavery in the Caribbean, but still it came as a bit of a shock! That said, I knew I was in safe hands as you'd worked on plays inspired by academic research before, including *Green Knight* and *The Remarkable Deliverances of Alice Thornton*, both written and performed by the amazing Debbie Cannon.

Flavia: That's right, you said that about the email! And I found out later that you were underselling yourself because you have written a thesis and had 20 years' experience commissioning and publishing research! It's funny how Professor Prest first approached me to join the Colonial-Era Caribbean Theatre and Opera Network (CECTON) as an early-career researcher when I was still doing my PhD and I didn't know about your academic background at the time. How did you feel when I told you that the play had been commissioned by a network of academics who wanted to draw attention to their research?

Catherine: I felt a sense of relief as that's essentially my role at the Scottish Government–to increase the impact of research, but I also felt an overwhelming sense of responsibility to represent the network's research accurately and, at the same time, to tell a compelling story, so my task was to find a delicate balance between facts and artistic licence. One of the first things I did was to write down what the overall purpose of the play was: to inform and to entertain. It was also helpful to have a clear brief and research material to draw on as the constraints did help me focus, especially given the limited timescale.

Flavia: You mentioned my previous work with Debbie Cannon on creating theatre from academic research for dissemination purposes, what I like to call 'Knowledge Exchange Theatre'. However, the pieces I'd worked on with Debbie were both more straightforward adaptations of one single source. Now with CECTON, we had papers from a whole network to sift through and use as source material for the play. Do you remember how you discovered the story of Minette?

Catherine: I really struggled to find a main character in the research articles, but fortunately Professor Prest had emailed me an article right at the start of the process, which discussed the life of a mixed-race opera performer known as 'Demoiselle Minette', and that of her white counterpart, Madame Marsan. I revisited the article, which reviewed fascinating evidence of Minette's operatic career in the late 1700s. Minette would have been classified as a *free woman of colour* irrespective of her outward appearance, which was likely fairly pale-skinned. Minette was described as absolutely compelling–she was clearly talented and successful, but as a free woman of colour, had a complex social status, and that's what made her fascinating.

Flavia: Indeed. I remember that the two of us and Jaïrus (Obayomi, dramaturg) were also taken with another one of Professor Prest's papers about runaway slave notices, which gave you the idea for Mama. What aspects of Minette or her mother's character resonate with you?

Catherine: Had I been around in the 1790s, I would have likely been put in the same social category as Minette, which really resonated with me and was quite jolting. Apart from both being mixed-race, however, Minette and I seem quite different—I can't sing a note for a start! I think I'm more like Mama, who was entirely my creation, drawing from a mixture of historical accounts of enslaved women (as scant as they are) and memories of my own family members. My Jamaican Nana was a huge influence on Mama's character and her unapologetic 'tough love' approach was something I remember vividly from childhood! This aspect of her character along which her dignified, upright posture and her quiet and uncompromising nature were instrumental in creating the character of Mama. However, it wasn't just the individual characters of Mama and Minette that resonated with me, it was the tense yet loving dynamic between them which was so familiar, and the fact they had both similar and very different experiences of oppression and racism.

Flavia: So, we began with these two characters, and then we set the scene. The idea for the title and the direction we would be going in came from the discussions about the lack of information about individual enslaved people, as the main takeaway from the first CECTON seminar we attended was how much was missing from the archives! We got together with Jaïrus for a first workshop to get some of your initial ideas on their feet, and I vividly remember the first exercise we did, when I asked you to visualise the theatre space and experiment with however many different beginnings for the play, and we eventually got to that opening line, 'I think I'm being watched'. Then it was a back-and-forth between trying things out in the rehearsal room and returning to the papers to enhance the details, but I was always extremely impressed at the speed at which you produced such high-quality, in-depth text! How did you find the process of creating *Placeholder*?

Catherine: Challenging! As I'm a researcher by trade, I did what felt natural to me so I reviewed the papers over and over, making extensive notes and supplementing with images, music, YouTube clips, basically everything relevant to the period I could find.

I recall that we found some of the research we read along the way pretty sobering. Discovering accounts of lived experiences of slavery was one of the most hard-hitting parts of the whole process and something you rarely read about in history textbooks. The real runaway slave notices that describe in detail the horrific injuries inflicted on enslaved people had an emotional impact on all of us. It was even more shocking to discover that these horrific notices are one of the very few sources which historians can draw on to get a glimpse into the lives of enslaved people. As a consequence, Jaïrus and I became very interested in what was *not* in the archives, the absence of experiences of slavery from an enslaved person's perspective was missing partly because of the nature of slavery itself, which silenced the voices of the victims of oppression. The terrible and enduring impact of these gaps in the archives became one of the central themes of the play.

To find a plot, I borrowed from my dayjob as a Government Analyst. I used a tool called a logic model or 'theory of change'. A theory of change is essentially an outcome-driven flow-diagram which enabled me to map out a logical pathway of scenes, dialogue and events, from the opening scene to the final scene.

Of all the investments, getting Jaïrus on board as our dramaturg was one of the most valuable. Instead of getting out her red pen, she asked me searching questions about the choices I'd made which really made me think about the purpose of every single line.

One of the most helpful parts of the process was the workshops you ran which explored how to create a solo piece focused on storytelling. Through exercises focusing on balance and movement you helped use my acting skills to experiment with playing both Mama and Minette just by using quick switches in posture and voice. Switching between the two characters made perfect sense given that Mama also represents Minette's political conscience.

Flavia: I also remember when Jaïrus advised you not to hold back putting whatever you wanted to put on the page, telling you not to worry about the staging, as that would be my job. In fact, we both encouraged you to make my directing job harder. What do you think we all learned from the first production of *Placeholder*?

Catherine: I have to thank The Edinburgh Multicultural Festival, the Being Human Festival and Professor Prest for giving us the opportunity to hold feedback sessions with the audience at the end of the first reading and the two performances. These were incredibly helpful for understanding how the play was received through the post-show discussions and, in a more formal manner, through structured questionnaires.

The feedback was overwhelmingly positive both regarding the audience feeling better informed about this period of history and the performance itself, which was hugely reassuring! One thing I wanted to change, however, was the balance between Mama and Minette's dialogue. Mama was clearly dominant, much more line-heavy, so I wanted to give Minette an important monologue near the end, which felt right both in terms of balancing the script but also in propelling the plot towards the conclusion. I also made some minor tweaks to the dialogue because you only really know how it flows when you're onstage!

Flavia: On that note, how would you describe the challenge of being both actor and playwright? How was writing for yourself?

Catherine: My acting experience was pretty helpful insofar that I could imagine how scenes might appear on the stage, especially as I was to perform them myself. Being the actor and the playwright also allows you to play to your strengths and avoid elements you find challenging... such as singing opera in my case! I was aware however, that I had to serve the story even if what I was asking the characters to do was out of my comfort zone, but I knew that you would direct the play in such a way that would support me to convey movements, accents, etc., even the ones I found tricky.

Flavia: I think this is why we work really well together, there is a lot of respect and understanding, but we also like to nudge each other over what we think is our limit. And here we are— your very first play, having come into this theatre world a little later in life than most people, without years of drama school training. I have told you countless times how proud I am but also how ridiculously unlikely this whole scenario is! Did you ever think you would have the play published?

Catherine With plays, often the main aim is to perform them rather than publish them, so publishing the script didn't cross my mind until Professor Prest asked if *Placeholder* could be used as a course text on the Political Theatre module at the University of St Andrews. I was over the moon that it was going to be used for educational purposes and this gave me a solid reason to seek a publisher, so I will be forever grateful to Salamander Street for agreeing to release Mama and Minette into the wild!

Flavia: It really is fantastic, and I hope our readers do enjoy connecting with these characters, learning from them, being moved by them! Of course, there is the play and there is the show. As a producer, I want the show to have a long life on stage beyond the two performances we have done so far, and as a director, I still want to tweak a couple of things as well. One of the reasons I love working with live theatre is its organic, responsive nature, which allows a show to be ever-changing. What would you say you want for *Placeholder* in the future?

Catherine: My goal for *Placeholder* is to continue to perform it to a range of audiences from all backgrounds which is why, where possible, I like that we try to ensure performances are either free of charge or priced as affordably as we can. I know you are in talks to take *Placeholder* to Paris and to the Caribbean and it would be an absolute dream to bring Minette and Mama home!

Placeholder

by Catherine Bisset

CHARACTERS

The play was conceived as a solo piece for an actress of Caribbean, African or mixed-race heritage with the actor playing both characters.

MINETTE:

A mixed-race opera singer. 30-35 years old. Minette's story is inspired by the life of an historical opera singer, Minette Ferrand, who performed in her home town of Port-au-Prince during the 1780s. At the time, she was one of only two people of colour performing on the public stage in Saint Domingue who we can name. The other is her half-sister Lise.

MAMA:

A fictional re-imagining of Minette's mother as an enslaved woman. 50-60 years old. Mama 'appears' to Minette but she is never physically present, but rather she is the voice of radical and political conscience. The character is depicted by the actress playing Minette who speaks 'in her mother's voice'.

1.

The stage is dark. MINETTE sits in the audience, in the last row at the back of the theatre. She greets and smiles politely as the audience comes in and take their seats.

There is a dressing table with a seat and a mirror SR. A pair of shoes is on the floor next to the dressing table, and an opera dress is draped over the seat. There is a single chair USC and a tailor's dummy SL, with a length of white fabric/skirt draped around the hips.

MINETTE: I do believe I'm being watched. I know some just come here to gossip, but nevertheless. Oh, the aroma in this place. It has a particular brutality to it, don't you think?

Well, I suppose hundreds of people in a theatre without facilities or any ventilation to speak of, yes, that will account for it.

And, personally, I would feel more comfortable if people sat a little bit further apart, after all this yellow fever is a real concern.

(*to an audience member*) Are you looking forward to the performance? I've heard he's a remarkable composer. Highly accomplished... considering.

And he's a Chevalier, no less.

(*MINETTE looks around the auditorium*)

Oh, look, there's the military taking their seats, and the boisterous ones? They're the lawyers, of course.

Oh, I love Madame Blanche's dress. Such a stunning shade of blue.

(*addresses the first audience member she interacted with*) Oh no, you don't think I'm here to watch the performance, do you? Oh, that's so very kind of you. Oh no, silly me I'm so sorry (*shakes head*) of course, you don't. The fact that I'm sitting in completely the wrong section gives me away, doesn't it. No, I'm just here to wait, not watch. No, please don't be concerned – as soon as

Madame arrives, I shall remove myself from this seat and go and stand in the back corridor with the others.

(*looks down at where the staring woman is sitting*)

I'm still being watched. (*slightly angry*) Perhaps she thinks I should consider this role demeaning. Well, I do not.

For a free person of colour, this is a perfectly respectable post.

Or perhaps she just thinks it is inappropriate for a woman to hold this position, after all, I am quite unique in that respect. I am very lucky indeed.

I treasure the opportunity to earn a life.

Oh no.

Oh dear, I meant to earn a living.

Earning a living and earning a life – they're not quite the same thing, are they? And oh, I could be a lot worse off. Oh, it could be a lot worse.

There are 500,000 people on this island who are not permitted to earn a living, so you see, I am extremely fortunate. Does that make me sound like a horrible person?

Oh, dear Lord, if my mother could hear me say that I was 'lucky' she'd be livid. I'd never hear the end of it. I can hear her say:

MAMA: (*VO*) 'Minette, the only reason they give out token freedoms on this island is to make you forget that you have no freedom at all'.

MINETTE: You see, my mother was brought from Jamaica to Saint Domingue in 1749, I believe, by– well– the Master she belonged to, of course, but she stubbornly refused to learn any French.

You might think that given that she's a sla–

Given her social status that she would go on at me about how lucky I was... but no, no, no, it's actually quite the contrary.

(*looks down to the row of front row seats*)

The woman is still staring. (*stands up*) No. Did she just point at me?!

MAMA: *(VO)* 'Now, now, now Minette − you're going to get yourself all irate. I know where all this is heading. Now you're going to over-explain again why you feel so, so grateful'.

MINETTE slowly and reluctantly moves down the auditorium stairs and moves on to the stage.

MINETTE: (*CS, facing the audience*) My sense of purpose is far stronger than anyone's disapproval.

Do you know what I feel when I wake up every morning?

Gratitude.

I'm grateful that I don't have to work in the fields, I'm grateful that I'm not a washerwoman with little dried-up twigs for fingers. In fact, I am thankful that I can own a domestic of my own and, yes, I'm thankful that I am not my mother.

There I said it. Honesty is another virtue that I treasure, because it is also such a rare and precious commodity here in Saint Domingue.

If I ever, ever feel even the slightest twinge of disappointment or malcontent, which is hardly ever, I remind myself that without pain, there is no courage.

The African workers on this island live for around three years, three − if they're lucky − so when you live here in Saint Domingue, even the tiniest privilege, well it matters because it can signify the difference between life and death.

Even just a glimpse of something beautiful, like a...

(pauses, searching for it)

...a tiny light shining through a tapestry, is worth grabbing onto just for that second.

I mean look, look up there, isn't that the most beautiful ceiling you've ever seen (*points to the ceiling*)?

Well, the Africans will never see that.

Never.

You must think I'm a horrible person. A coward? Selfish?

I'd understand if you thought that, and my mother would most likely agree with you.

(*spits this out*)

Why is that woman still looking at me?!

MINETTE transforms into MAMA. She takes a deep breath and slowly spins towards the tailor's dummy to let the MAMA 'mount'. MAMA speaks from behind the dummy.

MAMA: Minette, I'm sorry but my ears were burning.

You know why this woman watch you?

I know, and I'll tell you why.

MINETTE: Oh, Mother, I really do not need to hear this.

MAMA: Well, I tink different, my daughter.

MAMA lets her body react to drums.

So, you've heard that the rebel slaves are amassing in the hills of Saint Domingue, and the rebel drums are getting louder. They're getting angrier.

Now, the great white sharks on this island, they're afraid of the rebellion, but the smaller sharks, they're less terrified by the thought of an uprising than they are of... something else.

MINETTE: Oh, Mother. We all fear an uprising — I, for one, am dreading a war. If we just waited a bit longer for the legal challenge, we could avoid —

MAMA: No, no Minette, there's something far more threatening to these people than any war. *(looks into the audience)*

That woman, whose beady little eyes are burning a hole in your skull. Does she look like the kind of woman who tolerates shades of grey? Who is comfortable with... du-bi-ety?

No, no Minette. You see, her little war is making sure the likes of you don't get too close to the likes of her.

MINETTE: Are you seriously suggesting that, that woman sees me as a threat?

That woman?

That does not make any sense, Mother.

(she signals her mother to be quiet and moves away from the dummy towards DSR)

Shusssh! I think the performance is about to start. I hear he's a remarkable composer

MINETTE is about to step off the stage but is stopped by MAMA.

MAMA: Remember when I caught you rubbing lemon juice all over your skin? And I said to you, 'Minette – you could have a bath in the juice of 1000 lemons, but you ain't going to be nothing but brown!' *(laughs)* And I remember when you stuck dat ting on your head, what was it, a sheet or a skirt or something, me can't remember now, but you stuck it on your head, and you swished your head about like dis and said, 'look at my long blonde hair, Mama'. Oh, Damballa save us, you made me laugh!

MINETTE: Oh, Mother, why would you mention such a thing? I was six years old.

And see, that proves you wrong doesn't it! I was envious of her, not the other way around.

What do you think she was doing at six years old, smearing mud on her face to look like me? I hardly think so.

MAMA: Well, what you don't know is, while you were pretending to be a white person, Mistress Anxiety over there was swallowing soap to try to wash the creole out of her voice.

MINETTE: I still don't see what point you are trying to make.

Are you saying that this woman was not content with who she was?

Oh, wait. You're not seriously trying to suggest that she experienced some kind of anguish as a child, because I refuse to believe that woman has suffered a single day of her entire life.

MAMA: (*sighs*). No, dats not what I'm saying, Minette. What I'm saying is, this system puts us all in a cage. Your cage is bigger than my cage, and Mistress Anxiety's cage is just slightly larger than yours.

You know what your problem is?

MINETTE: (*sarcastically*) Oh, what a relief, I only seem to have one problem.

MAMA: If you choose to ignore what is ugly and what is brutal about this place, you hand your oppressors an extremely powerful weapon – your mind.

MAMA limps towards chair USC as she talks, sits down for a moment.

Do you remember when I told you the story of Yarico?

And none of your backchat Minette it is a true story... but you believed it was a tale of love. (*she chuckles*)

I had to explain to you that Yarico was betrayed by her lover when he sold her back into slavery to pay off his gambling debts, and, when he discovered she was carrying his child... he upped the price. Now, do you remember what you said – because I do?

(*switches to MINETTE's voice*) 'Well at least Yarico caught a glimpse of love and happiness in her tragic life.'

I mean c'mon, Minette!

You are very, very good at turning your head away from the painful truths of this world. But seeing the best in everything and everyone all the time is just a thin veil to cover up what's rotting underneath, and if you stay silent about your pain... they will hurt you and say you enjoyed it.

MAMA gets up and does chair score, eye contact with the audience.

8

Chair Choreography:

Startled by noise
goes on the ground
crawls behind chair, hiding
puts chair overhead, hiding
drags chair by foot to behind dummy / dressing table
uses the chair as shackles
walks to centre stage
gets beaten, lies over chair
crouches scared on chair,
stands on chair, holding neck
jumps off
MAMA puts the chair back in its original spot and sits down.

MAMA: Dat's all I'm trying to say.

Gets off chair, crouches next to it and addresses chair as MINETTE.

MINETTE: Mother, I need to ask you something.

When you ran away did you not give any consideration to what would happen to me, or what would happen to you if you were captured?

This was the third time, Mother. The third time!

Stands up as MAMA, limps DSC as she speaks the following lines...

MAMA: I didn't see it as running away. They call it running away. I was running *to* somewhere. In fact, me didn't even run, me walk most of the way, through the night and up into the mountainside, and I had a very particular destination in mind.

And no, I did not give any con-sid-er-ation to what would happen if I was caught, because if I had, I wouldn't have had the courage to do it.

MINETTE: I saw your runaway slave notice. It was in the Colonial Times. There you were.

9

Right next to the theatre announcements.

Walks towards dummy, removes shawl and drapes it around the shoulders of the dummy as she speaks the following...

Walks with a limp, branded with a Fleur de Lys on her right shoulder, both ears and hamstrings have been severed, last seen wearing a brown dress, 5 feet 4 inches tall. Those who know anything about these matters are asked to contact Monsieur Saint-Martin, director of the theatre in Port-au-Prince, to whom she belongs.

Takes a sidestep, looks the dummy up and down with disgust.

MAMA: Well, well... Tat is upsetting. Very upsetting...

Beat.

5 feet 4 - I'm taller than that!

Moves away from dummy as she speaks the following, stops DSR.

MINETTE: I'm glad you find it so amusing, Mother. Did you know that the authorities were convinced I was harbouring you? I insisted I had nothing to do with it, but they didn't believe me – they tore that plantation apart looking for you!

Madame was very, very angry. Oh, she was so angry.

It wasn't brave, Mother. Such a stupid, dangerous, selfish thing to do! But you didn't care, did you? You gave no thought to the consequences and no thought to how it would affect me, my life, did you? Did you?!

Uncomfortable pause. Moves only the head up, takes in the auditorium as MAMA.

MAMA: You know me never been in a theatre before. Me love all dem fancy decorations but Lord have mercy it's hotter than Hell in here!

And wat is dat stench? It smell like diseased sweat and human waste. (*looks at 'Mistress Anxiety' who is in the audience*). Human waste is right.

Still, I'd love to sit my black behind right down there in the front row in the middle of the white section and hear what our music sounds like in a place like dis.

Oh, we could get up on that stage down there and show dem people how to dance.

MAMA dances, plays with the audience, gets them to clap along, and takes up the entire stage.

Music stops and MINETTE interrupts the dancing.

MINETTE: Oh, you know what I'd love to do? I'd love to host one of those great balls. I would invite all the ladies on the island, well, the respectable ones, and I'd dance as they dance. I'd dance all night long.

MAMA: What ya talking about Dancing? Dem ball people can't dance! They just walk up and down with their hand stuck up in the air (*mimics the posh dancing*) – Dat is not dancing, Minette. These white people got no sense of rhythm. They scared a dancing in case their wig fall off.

Limps to dressing table, moves the dress from dressing table stool to chair USC as she speaks the following..

Oh, Minette. You know how much me love our music and our dancing but what I cannot stand are dem, what are dey called Minette? Dem plays. People pretendin to be other people, I can't abide it. I saw one of dem once and me never ever want to see it again.

MINETTE: Why? What did you see?

MAMA: (*sits down at the dressing table, speaks to the audience*) Well, me can't remember how old I was now - nine, ten - someting like that. My Mistress had invited a group of travelling performers to come to the plantation. Oh, Minette, I was so excited to catch a glimpse of the show - I hid behind a door and I waited, and I waited, but then me saw something that made me realise what my Mistress really thought of me. What the white people really thought of me.

'An actor - a white man, but his whole face was black, Minette - his whole body was black, painted black! And he wasn't singing...

He was screeching, shrieking, his eyes all popping out of his head. And I knew - I knew that he was mocking me. And the audience - they laughed, and they clapped and they cheered.

In my young child's mind I truly believed that the white man had take possession of the black man - like the devil himself he'd slipped inside him and could make him do whatever he wanted him to do.

And what the white man wanted him to do was make a fool of himself, so when all dem people went back to their plantations they were reminded that we weren't quite human.

Looks in the mirror, does the next lines to the mirror, adjusting the mirror at different angles or examining her face, touching and tugging at the skin...

I stayed silent, of course. It wasn't my place to ask questions or criticise.

My Mistress was kind compared to some, Minette. But from that day I knew dat woman just saw me as empty. Like an empty water jug - I had no soul. I had no religion. I felt no pain. I was just a ting to be worked to death. And because I was empty, she could stuff me to the brim with dat damn religion of hers.

A religion made for a slave Mistress - where she falls to her knees in her silk skirt to beg for a Kingdom in the sky because what she stole from me, still isn't enough! Den I hear her beg her Lord for his forgiveness. But she never begged me for mine.

Sometimes, I hear the slaves talking, and dem saying 'oh my Mistress kind. She don't beat me, she don't whip me, she treat me nice'

Well, you know what I say?

A cage made of the finest gold is still a cage.

(*looks back to the audience and locks eyes on 'Mistress Anxiety'*) So your watcher down there, the one in the enormous white wig?

Her name is Madame de Laurent. She married a very rich man. Two plantations, 300 slaves and, if you look close, you'll see a tiny mark, right here (*points to temple*) because one of her slaves tell me she got a little tired of being shoved around.

She's white, of course – but born here, raised in Saint Domingue, so not a great white shark - they call her a 'petit blanc' and she know her place.

I don't call her dat, Minette, that's what the Code Noir calls her. Dat's her status.

The reward for her capture? (*scoffs*) There isn't enough gold in the world.

Dat woman is cruel, Minette, but at least is only looking at you with evil intent – because you don't even want to know what she does to her slaves.

MINETTE: Well, I can see now why I crawl under her skin, but what I do not understand is why she's so rude, staring at me like that! Wasn't she ever taught any manners? I just find her behaviour – crushingly disappointing.

MAMA: Ha! Funny you should say dat.

Stands up, grabs the wig and limps towards DSL where Mme de Laurent is sitting and addresses the audience on that side.

The high-class white women on dis island think she has atrocious social manners. Because she's a creole, like you - born here, raised here. They tink she is undereducated, crass, unable to hold sophisticated conversation, and dare I say it... Some of dem believe - dat she almost black (*laughs loudly*). So no wonder she despises you!

If she can't be better than a free person of colour, who can she be better than?

MINETTE: (*smoothing out the wig, as if MAMA had messed it up*) Oh, I understand.

I just wondered, well, I was hoping that she was staring at me because she recognised me from my past? When I was a si... (*tails off*)

But it seems I am very much mistaken.

MAMA: What is your greatest disappointment, Minette?

MINETTE: Where did that come from? What do you mean? I really do not want to discuss this.

MAMA: Remember what I said about being silent about your pain. Why did you stop, Minette?

MINETTE: (*angrily*) If I choose to be silent, I will be.

MAMA: But I don't understand why you would make that choice any more than I understand why are you sitting here holding a seat for some white woman when you don't have to be!

MINETTE: I really don't want to talk about it, Mother.

MAMA: Was it anything to do with Mistress Anxiety by any chance or at least the likes of her?

Did somebody say something to you?

Do something to you?

MINETTE: There was simply no point, no point whatsoever in carrying on, and this is as close to a stage as I ever want to get, now please, Mother – that's enough!

Angrily throws the wig to the floor.

MAMA: I'm just trying my best to understand what happened, Minette.

Moves away from the dummy, stops CS. Addresses dummy/MAMA as she speaks.

MINETTE: (*seething*) Why? Why do you care? You just think I'm an imbecile who understands precisely nothing. You just think I'm ashamed, don't you? Ashamed of who I am, ashamed of who you are and ashamed of feeling grateful? Ashamed! Ashamed! Ashamed!

Why should I feel shame?

I can't help what I am, Mother, any more than you can't help what you are, so don't you dare try to make me feel guilty for something over which I have absolutely no control!

MAMA: You're a far more obedient slave than I am, Minette.

MINETTE: Oh, you were always amusing, Mother. I am a free woman of colour! Frec. Oh, that's not what I call myself.. That's what the Code Noir calls me.

That. is. my. status!

MAMA: Do you know who make the best slaves, Minette? Those who believe they are free.

Beat.

MINETTE: I am perfectly content with who I am now, no matter what you think. And you could never comprehend that anyone else might have suffered, least of all me.

Oh, I know exactly what you're going to say, but you must know this – I may have never been struck by a whip, Mother, but there are many other ways that this island can beat the life out of you.

Do you even know who is performing this evening?

MAMA: You've said he was a remarkable composer.

Highly accomplished.

Well. ... - Considering...?

MINETTE: Yes. Yes.

I'll tell you about him, shall I?

Not that it really matters.

His name is - No - They call him The Chevalier de Saint Georges. He is the Conductor of the leading symphony orchestra, not just in the whole of Paris, Mother, but in the whole of Europe.

And that's not all... A Virtuoso violinist. A champion Fencer. And oh, so handsome. So charming - I hear he is a favourite of the Queen.

In fact, he is everything Herr Mozart is not and yet they call The Chevalier - The Black Mozart.

The thing is, Mother, I read recently that Herr Mozart-

- yes, Mother, the white one –

– has just completed a new composition which contains within it a completely unique and exciting musical gesture. It's a particularly difficult sequence of string notes which climbs to the higher register of the instrument and then falls dramatically.

Oh, Mother, the critics were so excited. He's extraordinary, they say. C'est un génie! Très bien, Herr Mozart. Magnifique! Formidable!

MINETTE claps mockingly.

But what I happen to know is that a whole year before Mozart even conceived of that piece, the Chevalier performed his violin concerto and within it contained-

MAMA: Don't tell me.

The exact same musical gesture?

MINETTE: Very good, Mother.

A remarkable coincidence, don't you think?

And yet, they still call him, the Chevalier, The Black Mozart.

And I can't even remember his real name.

MINETTE moves to chair USC, picks up the dress, looks at it, sits down and drapes the dress across her lap. MINETTE strokes/smooths out and caresses the dress.

MINETTE: My sister and I were the only free women of colour performing on the public stage in Saint Domingue - the only ones. I sang with the Opera-Comique and I excelled.

In fact, I was ready to take on one of the most demanding roles in the repertoire - That of Nina. Now, my singing ability was exemplary but this role required formidable acting skills too, so I'd been working so so hard. So hard.

Oh, I had a lot to live up to. You see, the great Madame Marsan had already played the role of Nina, and she was magnificent. Critics adored her and audiences loved her – You see, she had a very special gift. She was able to transport the audience all the way back to Paris simply by altering the tone and the pitch of her voice – Quite extraordinary. And of course, the audiences in Saint Domingue loved that, because, well, many of them were homesick.

I had the privilege of performing alongside Madame Marsan. Just the secondary roles of course - Peasants and Villagers and the like. I think because I was young. But I was ready now - I was ready to play Nina....

(*stops stroking the dress*) And then I read a critic's review of one of my performances that made me realise that there really was no point, Mother, because I now understood what white people really thought of me.

Oh, this critic was much more subtle than your black-faced actor, Mother, but to me what he said was as brutal as the stench in this place.

I'll tell you what he wrote, shall I?

Stands up, takes the dress with her DSC, critic's VO plays, she stares at the audience. Uses dress as a puppet, pretending to be the critic speaking.

CRITIC V/O: 'First, we would have to applaud the soul, the intelligence, the finesse, the kindness, of a young Creole Actress, who would be toasted, even in Paris...'

VO stops. Lowers dress briefly and moves into the light to speak MAMA's line.

MAMA: And you're complaining?

MINETTE moves back into the shade, and moves dress/puppet again, VO resumes.

CRITIC V/O: 'However, we would invite her to declaim the dialogue less, to tire herself less to pronounce purely, to dress better sometimes in the roles of Peasants; to overload oneself less with gauze, ribbons and taffeta; because not only displaced and ridiculously puffy adornments contrast with the roles of Villagers, but they often make her seem like a pretty small bust placed on a huge pedestal.'

VO ends. MINETTE only holds and admires the dress as she speaks.

MINETTE: Oh, I know, it just sounds like constructive criticism doesn't it, but you and I, Mother, you and I know what he really meant don't we?   (*MINETTE mimics the critic's voice*) 'Know your place.'
'Who do you think you are dressing in those fine clothes, they're not for the likes of you.'
'You have no right, they're not for your class, dear. You see, you are just a peasant.'
'You're small.'
'You're worthless'
'You're nothing.'

Lets the dress drop on the floor and waits for a second.

So you see, there really was no point. I knew that they'd never really hear my voice, would they? There would always be... something.
And did you notice? That critic didn't even bother to quote my name in that review, so not only was I inappropriate, but I was completely invisible.

(*MINETTE looks over at the tailor's dummy*) Oh, I can tell by your face you think I'm a ridiculous person. Spoilt? Selfish?

Oh, I know. I mean it's really just about my clothes isn't it, Mother? It's just a stupid costume! Hardly important in the grander scheme of things!

Maybe. Maybe... But don't you ever tell me that I can't see what's rotting underneath! Because I do.

Oh, I do.

As MAMA, picks up the dress off the floor and puts it on dummy as she speaks the following lines...

MAMA: That is not what my face says at all, Minette. Dats dem trying to stamp you down – just the same as Mistress Anxiety over there is trying to do – they're just trying to intimidate you.

But what I do not understand is why are you letting them? Why are you giving into dem, Minette?

If you want to play Nina, then you play her. And if you want to go on stage wearing the biggest ball gown on this island made of the finest silk, then you do it while you still can, *(limps over to dressing table, picks up shoes)* because I happen to know that the law now states that the free people are no longer allowed to wear shoes- That's how much you threaten them, Minette. And that's how much they envy you.

Well, you know what I say, Minette? You go and buy yourself a pair of sandals and you adorn your feet with diamonds and get back up on that stage and you sing for your life because that is what resistance looks like, Minette!

Puts shoes on dressing table.

You use those small freedoms you have but never ever feel grateful for them – do you do understand me? You use them to climb as high as you can because there are 500,000 souls on this island who can't even take a piss without permission – so you owe it to them!

MINETTE: *(sobbing)* I am nothing like you! I don't have the courage, Mother.

MAMA: Without pain there is no courage, isn't that what you said? So you must use your pain to find your courage, Minette, because if you refuse to move, you will never notice your chains!

MINETTE: You know when I felt pain. No, no it wasn't pain – it was shame.

When I saw your runaway notice. It reminded me that my own mother was just... chattel.

Not even a human being according to the law. My own mother. And then when you were captured, the shame I felt was unbearable.

I'm so sorry, Mother. I'm so, so sorry.

Please forgive me.

MAMA: We live on an island when simply wanting to be a human being is a crime, but beating one to death is not.

And you don't really believe dat what I did was the crime, do you, Minette?...

And of course you felt ashamed, that's what they want you to feel, because if the free people of colour despise the Africans as much as they do - that makes them stronger and us weaker... but don't you ever forget that they only call you 'free' because you'd shame your father – because he couldn't have a child who was a... slave, could he? That would never do.

And her, over there.

How do you think she sees me? Sees this collar around my neck?

MINETTE: Oh, I'm sure you don't need me to tell you that.

MAMA: No, you're right, Minette, I don't. But you see, that's her mistake, because she should see me as a warning, because accordin to The Code Noir we are both worth less than dey are, and come to think of it so are you. And when push come to shove greed sees no colour so you both better pray they don't run out of Africans.

So your social position is not fortunate, Minette. It is precarious. So you must resist in any way you can. Don't let them rip your wings from your body the way they have torn them from mine. So you get up on that stage and you sing until they drag you from it!

MINETTE: Why does any of this even matter when a war is coming Mother? What you don't seem to understand is the rebellion doesn't stand a chance against the might of the French army. They will be crushed. Don't you even care that thousands of people will die?!

Pushes shoes off dressing table onto the floor.

There has never been a successful slave revolt. Never. And when the rebellion is defeated can you even imagine what they'll do to us then?

No.

A rebellion is not to be supported.

It will only lead us into a world of unimaginable terror and suffering.

And even if by some miracle the uprising was successful, do you really believe that the majority of white people on this island will accept a black republic? Never, never.

MAMA: The majority of white people? What you talkin' about, majority? Majority don't mean a damn thing on this island, Minette. – I am the majority!

And a lie doesn't become truth, wrong does not become right, and evil does not become good, just because it's accepted by a majority!

But you're right about one thing: Most likely all of us will die. But if the African slaves and the free people can unite, we might just stand a slim chance. What was it you said? A tiny light shining through a tapestry is worth grabbing onto just for that second, remember?

Picks up one shoe at a time off the floor and limps towards the dummy, carrying shoes as she speaks the following lines...

You know, the thought of dying never bothered me much.

In fact, most of the time I would beg for it.

But what did vex me was the thought of being forgotten.

Slavery has stolen our names. Our language. Our culture. Our children. Our *pride*. Our humanity. But it was not just to control us, Minette. It was to erase us - Silence us, so we can never tell our side of the story and I believe *that* is a greater act of violence than even slavery itself.

Stops by the dummy for a moment, addresses the following back to MINETTE.

But you - You and this remarkable composer - Your lights shine so brightly that the history books cannot ignore you. And if you can leave a trace behind, we will be found. They will find us.

MAMA puts shoes down by the dummy and faces the audience.

MINETTE: I'm not sure we will be found, Mother. Are you forgetting that that critic didn't even mention me by name, and I still can't remember the real name of the Chevalier.

They'll just say whatever they want to say about us, Mother, do whatever they want to us. They will tear us down or ignore us completely and there's nothing we can do about that.

MAMA: Of course they will try to tear you down, try to diminish you, but they can't ignore you completely, Minette.

Are you forgetting what that critic person actually wrote? He said that he applauds your soul, your intelligence, your finesse, your kindness, and he said you will be toasted in Paris, remember?

Minette, they couldn't ignore you if they tried. Don't you understand yet... You are the light that shines through the tapestry Minette – It's you

(*limps to CS*) You want Mistress Anxiety over there writing your history?

How about the likes of your father? The enslaver. The rapist?

And what about my history? - The only proof I ever existed as a human being is that damn runaway slave notice. And that can't even get my height right...

But you. You can be remembered. And not just as some Placeholder sitting in a chair for some white woman, but as a human being with talent, finesse, intelligence, and kindness, as somebody with something to say. And above all, as a woman with courage.

Limps to dressing table.

You know when I was a washerwoman, I noticed something. My Mistress - all dem Mistresses - were obsessed with keeping everything white - linen, tablecloths, underskirt, everyting. So dey made us scrub and scrub with lemon juice, until our finger shrivelled into – What did you call dem? Twigs? (*looks at her fingers and chuckles*) That's right.

So, you know what I used to do?

She rubs finger on rouge in makeup box on the table, then wipes it on her white skirt.

I used to leave a tiny mark on every single one of them – Oh, I know it sound crazy. But when I saw how enraged they were - at something so tiny - I realised that leaving a mark that they can't wash out is the most powerful form of resistance of all.

Beat.

MINETTE: (*in spotlight, to the audience*) It was my first performance in this theatre - on that very stage. I was trembling so much I almost fainted. As a solo violin played the overture, I opened my mouth but - no sound came out. The violin stopped and then it started again but I was completely paralyzed. I could not sing. I gazed upwards into the distance, towards the boxes where the people of colour were seated in the second tier. They were all crammed together, it seemed, not a hair between them and then I saw it for the first time - they were bonded to each other in resolute, unwavering solidarity, and they were waiting, too.

The violin started again and I tried to recover my composure but there was such distress in their eyes it made me want to scream. And then I heard your voice, Mama. And you whispered: (*in MAMA's voice*) Your voice is your weapon and you're going to use it. The violin went quiet for a second time. Then it hit the chord again and the orchestra craned its neck towards the stage. I looked up again, and this time my voice rang out, a vibrato so crystal clear that I could hear the audience gasp in admiration. Everything else vanished; the theatre, the orchestra, and even the boxes on the second tier where the free people were seated - exhausted and broken - and willing me to sing.

MAMA: We may not be the makers of our own history...

MINETTE: ...but we are made by it.

MAMA: Minette. What use are your freedoms?...

MINETTE: If I am not equal...

MAMA: If we are not equal...

MINETTE: Gratitude. Gratitude? That's what they need me to feel.

So I stay shackled to this seat, for the rest of my life.

Short beat.

But, can I earn a life again?
Can I make a mark?

MAMA: And wear diamonds on your feet. Yes, you can, Minette.

MINETTE: I do not have your courage, Mother, but... I think I can find enough to do that.

MAMA: You must treasure the opportunity to *earn* a life, Minette.

And if you need any final words of encouragement from your mother, I can guarantee you that nothing would make...

Short beat.

... me prouder...

Beat.

...than to hear your voice again.

MINETTE: (*gasps as if MAMA has left her. Walks to the chair, sits down and addresses the audience*) Are you looking forward to the performance? He is a remarkable composer. He leads the most accomplished orchestra in the whole of Europe. Oh, his name? You know the strange thing is I can't quite remem...

No wait. I do remember.

His name is Joseph Bol -

MAMA begins to limp off the stage, gets down and speaks the final lines from the floor in front of the stage.

MAMA: (*cuts MINETTE off*) Oh, no, no, no, Minette.

MAMA limps to centre stage and fixes her gaze to the back of the theatre where MINETTE was sitting at the start.

Now you get out of that seat and you leave this theatre and you do not come back until you are on that stage.

Beat.

And I will be here. Every. Single. Night. With my black behind in the front row in the middle of the white section...

Long-ish beat.

Now go.

MAMA's eyes are fixed on the back row of the auditorium where MINETTE had been sitting at the start of the play and they follow MINETTE as she leaves the theatre. MAMA smiles and she takes a seat in the front row.

THE END

POSTSCRIPT

In August 1791, at a secret vodou ceremony, the signal was given for the uprising to begin. Enslaved people throughout the northern province of Saint-Domingue turned on their white landowners, and thousands were killed. After a bitter conflict of over 12 years, the former colony was declared independent on 1st January 1804. Renamed Haiti, the western portion of Hispaniola became the first independent Black nation in the Western Hemisphere and the revolution became a catalyst for the eventual collapse of the Transatlantic Slave Trade.

ALSO AVAILABLE FROM SALAMANDER STREET

All Salamander Street plays can be bought in bulk at a discount for performance or study. Contact info@salamanderstreet.com to enquire about performance liscences.

Chatsky and Miser, Miser! by Anthony Burgess

Paperback ISBN: 9781914228889
eBook ISBN: 9781914228308

Anthony Burgess expertly tackles the major monuments of French and Russian theatre: *The Miser* by Molière and *Chatsky* by Alexander Griboyedov. Burgess's recently discovered verse and prose plays are published for the first time in this volume.

King Hamlin by Gloria Williams
ISBN: 9781739103033

In a maze of inequality, unemployment and gang culture, it's a struggle to know where to make a right turn and how to undo a wrong one. Hamlin, Quinn and Nic are young friends trying to get ahead in inner city London.

Outlier by Malaika Kegode
ISBN: 9781914228339

Genre-defying and emotional, *Outlier* explores the impact of isolation, addiction and friendship on young people.

CRISIS: The Theatre Responds by Carol Rocamora

Paperback ISBN: 9781914228308
eBook ISBN: 9781914228735

Exploring the courageous playwrights of the world who used the stage as a platform to address crises of the 20th and 21st centuries. From Bertolt Brecht to present day playwrights, Carol Rocamora discusses how theatre has addressed crises from World War II to the present, including war, apartheid, communism, authoritarianism, racism, immigrant and refugee issues, environmental peril and the pandemic.

9 781914 228919